NICOLE VISITS AN AMISH FARM

A Photo Story by Erika Stone

Text by Merle Good

Nicole Visits an

Amish

Farm

WALKER AND COMPANY New York, N.Y.

Dedicated to
the many tens of thousands
of children who visited and hosted
and learned from each other

Library of Congress Cataloging in Publication Data

Stone, Erika.   Good, Merle
Nicole visits an Amish farm.

Summary: A young city dweller experiences homesickness as well as
happiness during her two-week stay with Amish farmers who live in
Pennsylvania.
   1.Amish—Pennsylvania—Social life and customs—Juvenile literature.
2. Farm life—Pennsylvania—Juvenile literature. 3. Pennsylvania—Social
life and customs—Juvenile literature. 4. Fresh-air charity—Pennsylvania—Juvenile literature. [1. Amish. 2. Farm life] I. Good, Merle,
ill. II. Title.
F160.M45S8 1982   974.8'0088287   81-23085
ISBN 0-8027-6444-4   AACR2

First published in the United States of America in 1982 by the Walker
Publishing Company, Inc.

Published simultaneously in Canada by John Wiley & Sons Canada, Lim-
ited, Rexdale, Ontario.

This edition printed in 1985.

Printed in the United States of America

10 9 8 7 6 5 4 3 2

Book designed by Lena Fong Hor

NICOLE VISITS AN AMISH FARM

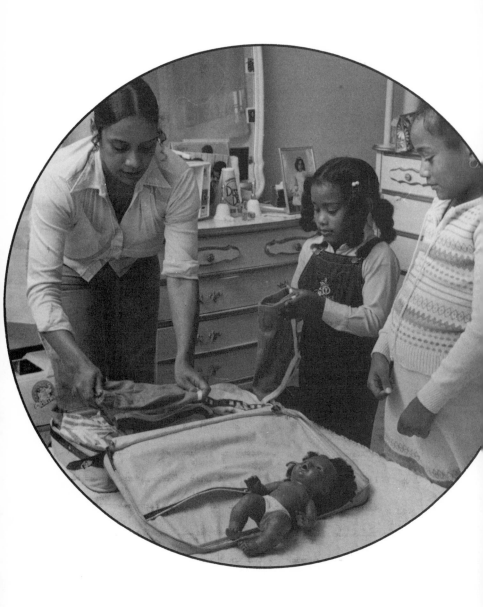

Nicole's family didn't have money for a summer vacation this year, so they were happy when she was invited to the country to visit with an Amish family on their farm in Pennsylvania. Her mother and father told her there would be few cars there and no television.

When Nicole got off the bus in Lancaster, she was greeted by a woman wearing a brown dress and a white head covering. Her young daughter was with her.

"Are you Nicole?" the girl asked.

Nicole nodded.

"I'm Charity," the girl said. "You're coming to stay with us, Nicole," she added with a shy smile.

Nicole liked Charity right away. She was friendly.

When they got to the farm, Nicole took off her shoes and dug her toes into the soft earth. The air smelled so good.

Charity took Nicole to meet the animals. The black and white cows chewed in a friendly sort of way. And Nicole adored their baby calves.

Charity showed her tiny baby chicks, only two days old. Nicole smiled as she touched the soft down and felt the scratchy feet of one of the chicks.

Nicole was hungry. She was glad when Charity's mother called them for supper. At the table she met the rest of Charity's family—her two older brothers, two younger sisters, and baby brother.

After supper the girls went for a ride in Uncle Levi's black and gray buggy. The horse's name was Hurricane.

"Does he bite?" Nicole asked.

Charity laughed. "No, he's as tame as can be. Get in. Let's go!"

They rode down a narrow lane, through a covered bridge, and past cornfields and pretty brick farmhouses. Everything was quiet as Hurricane clip-clopped past the fields and meadows. New York City seemed far away.

The sun wasn't even up yet when Nicole woke up the next morning. She and Charity dressed quickly and hurried to the barn. The morning air was chilly.

Hundreds of chickens cackled as the sun came up. Snappermouth, the dog, barked at the girls as they ran into the cow stable.

The girls rested on the barnyard fence to watch Charity's brother feed the heifers. The biggest, Huckleberry, marched over and tried to lick them. "It's not nice to stick your tongue out," Charity scolded Huckleberry. The girls laughed.

The pigs were not as friendly. They hooted their snouts and scurried around squealing so loudly that they scared Nicole.

Then Nicole met Charity's cat, Shusslick. Her name comes from Pennsylvania Dutch, a special language the Amish use. It's a mixture of German and English. Sometimes it was hard for Nicole to understand it. "Shusslick" means someone who hurries too fast and trips over his own feet.

Shusslick wiggled when Nicole held her, and purred a welcome.

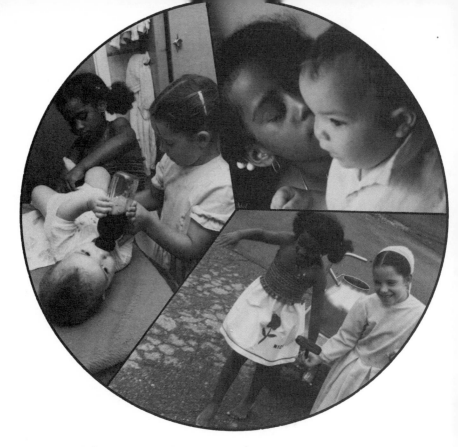

After breakfast Nicole helped Charity care for her baby brother, Michael. They rocked Michael in the big rocker and gave him his bottle. In big families, older children learn to help the younger ones.

Working together is important on the farm. Everyone is needed. Chores become enjoyable because everyone helps.

"I like helping with Michael most of all," Charity said.

The next day Charity took Nicole to see her school. It was locked for the summer, so they played outside on the see-saw and the swings.

"All grades sit in the same room, and we all have the same teacher," Charity explained.

"One of my favorite subjects is German," Charity said. "And we sing a lot of songs in German," she added. "But I hate arithmetic."

Charity and Nicole got a drink at the water pump. "My school has four floors and many rooms," Nicole told Charity. "I don't think I'd like such a little school."

When they got home they visited Charity's grandmother, who had her own little home attached to the family's big farmhouse. "That way, we can take care of her if she needs us," Charity explained.

Grandma served the girls homemade fudge and cold lemonade. Then she showed them an old book which had a family tree beautifully written inside its cover. It listed the names of Charity's relatives. "My mother has a book like this," Nicole said. "And I saw a man on TV show how to make a family tree."

Charity's grandmother
smiled. Then Nicole remembered that they had no television.

That afternoon Charity's
mother took the girls to a
country store to buy fabric to
make Nicole a dress.

Nicole learned to thread a needle as her dress
was being cut and sewn together. It was an Amish
dress, long like Charity's, but lavender instead of
green. The Amish wear simple and modest
clothes.

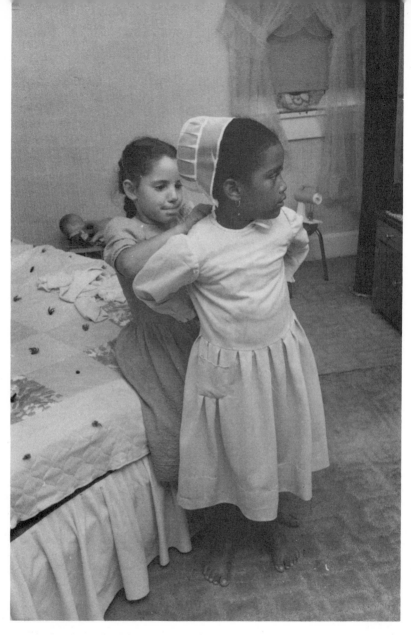

Later that day Nicole took off her Amish dress. "I don't want to stay here anymore," she said. "I want to go home."

Nicole sat in the swing under the big tree and started to cry. She missed her parents, her mother's cooking, her daddy's laughter, her sister's teasing, and the noise of the city. But more than anything, she missed television. And sometimes she felt confused when Charity's family spoke in the Pennsylvania Dutch language and she didn't understand.

"Why don't you write a letter to your family," Charity's mother suggested. "Tell them how you feel."

So Nicole wrote a long letter home. She told all about Charity and her family, the farm, the quiet nights, the pigs and cows, the buggy ride, and the garden. She mentioned Shusslick, Snappermouth, and Hurricane. She forgot about Huckleberry.

Charity walked with her to the end of the lane. They put the letter in the mailbox and put the flag up so the mailman would know it was there.

Nicole felt much better.

That night they lay on the patchwork quilt which Charity's mother had made and told stories. Nicole told Charity all about the city, about the noise and dirt, the subways and the buses, her school, the playground, and her favorite park for swimming.

"Daddy took us to see the Mets play baseball last year," she said. But Charity didn't know much about baseball.

Soon they were tired of talking so they crayoned until bedtime in coloring books Nicole had brought.

Amish families raise most of their own food. Their gardens provide vegetables. The cows give them milk. The chickens provide eggs. The bees make honey, and the orchard trees produce apples and cherries and pears.

Charity's family tended two gardens. The vegetables in the large one, called the "truck patch," were for selling—sweet corn, four rows of lima beans and green beans, a row of potatoes with blossoms, and a row of leafy sweet potatoes.

The garden near the house had short tidy rows

of carrots, cabbage, cucumbers, radishes, red beets, and flowers. Nicole helped Charity pick cucumbers. They used their dresses for baskets, and Nicole picked a big bouquet of zinnias for Charity's mother.

Nicole helped to husk sweet corn for lunch. She learned to pull off the husk around the ear of corn and brush away the silk. Then she watched Charity's mother cook it. Charity's mother called it "roastin' ears." Nicole's mother called it "corn-on-the-cob."

On wash day Nicole helped pump the water and Charity helped wash the clothes. Nearly all of the clothing for the family had been made by Charity's mother and grandmother. Together the girls

helped Charity's sister hang the garments on the line to dry. Most Amish families use washing machines to do their laundry, but Charity's family used a tub sometimes.

Aunt Elizabeth came to help prepare canned peaches. It was a big job. They split open the peaches, peeled them, put them in glass jars, and cooked them in the jars in boiling water. "That way, we'll have good eating next winter," Aunt Elizabeth explained. "It's an old way of keeping food tasty."

They carried the jars down to the basement, and Charity's brother put them on high shelves.

The following day Charity's father and brother cut and baled a field of hay. By noon there were black clouds in the sky.

"I'm afraid it will rain tonight," Charity's father said. So everyone went out to help load the hay onto the wagons.

"Let's not be too doplick," Charity's brother said, half laughing and half serious.

"That means clumsy," Charity explained.

They climbed onto the hay wagon and threw
the bales down to Aunt Elizabeth. She put them
on a hay elevator which took them high inside the
barn where Charity's father stacked them for the
winter. The bales were large and bulky, but not as
heavy as they looked.

Many Amish farmers use modern farm equipment so they can produce plentiful crops. But others work their farms with horses and old-fashioned equipment.

The sky clouded over, but the rain did not come and they got the hay into the barn safely.

The girls danced on the empty wagon. "Let's go swimming!" Charity said, as the sun came out from behind the clouds.

Nicole loved to swim. She showed Charity her best stroke, and taught her how to float on her back.

There was a big windmill beside the pond. Nicole listened to it creak as it turned in the breeze. "It supplies power to the pump." Charity said. "That's how we get water into our homes and barns."

After supper, Nicole and Charity helped wash and dry the dishes. Then Charity showed Nicole some beautiful old dishes in a cupboard. "Some of these belonged to my great grandmother," she said. "We don't use them. We just look at them."

"They're pretty," Nicole said.

"Would you like to play checkers?" Charity asked.

"No, I don't feel like it," Nicole answered.

So the girls got out a big box of paper dolls and played for a while. Charity's family had plenty of fun without a radio or television. The children invented games and played together. On some warm evenings they played outside—Hide-and-Seek, Kick-the-Can, Bag-Tag, Fox-and-Geese. And when it got dark, they sat in the swing and told stories to scare one another.

But on this evening, as they did almost every evening, Charity's family read the Bible together and sang hymns and songs in the parlor. It was a special time. And just before they went to bed, Charity's father sang, "Schluf, Buble, Schluf." It means "Sleep, Baby, Sleep." Nicole felt happy and homesick at the same time.

A new calf was born in the barn the next morn-

ing. They watched its mother help it to stand and walk. "That's almost magical," Nicole said.

The cows and heifers were eating outside the barn. One of the bigger calves came and sucked Charity's hand. "Try it," Charity told Nicole. "The calf likes it."

But Nicole didn't like the idea. "Yuk," she squealed as she backed away.

That night Charity's cousins came. They had a
city visitor on their farm, too. They all sat at the
table enjoying many servings of salads, meats,
vegetables, breads and rolls, and **five** desserts.
"It's what we call wonderful good cooking," Charity's uncle explained. "We want to make sure you
42   come back next summer."

It was Nicole's last full day on the farm. The girls had many things they wanted to do. "Let's go swimming again. Let's go see Grandma. Let's make homemade ice cream. Let's ride in the buggy," Nicole said at breakfast. Charity's mother laughed.

They romped in the hayfield behind the corn barn until Nicole's feet got sore and Charity had

to pretend to carry her. They climbed the tree above the swings and Nicole stubbed her toe.

The girls had gotten up early so that Nicole could say goodbye to the cows, the new calf, the pigs, the chickens, the ducks, Shusslick and Snappermouth and Hurricane. And Hornet, the bull Charity's father had just bought.

Charity's mother took them to the station where the bus was waiting. The girls put their arms around each other.

"Will we meet again?" Nicole asked.

 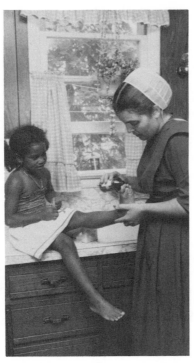 

"Sure," Charity smiled. "I'll come to see you someday in the city. Maybe we can even go to the zoo."

Nicole nodded. "Maybe I can come back next year." She felt sad. She had had a good time with Charity and her family. She had learned about the Amish people and their ways. She hated to leave.

Then Nicole remembered her mother and daddy and her sister waiting for her in New York. Suddenly she could hardly wait to see them. It was good to be going home.

More About The Amish

There are more than 90,000 Amish living in seventeen different states and one province of North America. Their population has more than doubled in the last two decades.

Their beginnings date from the time of the Anabaptist movement in Europe (1525) during the Protestant Reformation. They were called **Mennonites** after one of their leaders, Menno Simons, a former Catholic priest from the Netherlands. A hundred and fifty years later, in 1693, a group of Mennonites, led by Jacob Amman, broke away from the Mennonite fellowship. Amman's followers were nicknamed **Amish**. The Mennonites and the Amish continue to be spiritual cousins.

The Amish people believe their faith in God affects everything they do. Staying together as a community and being faithful Christians are top priorities. The principle issue of concern within Amish communities is this: **How does one live a holy life and pass along one's values of Christian community to one's children?**

It isn't easy. It takes effort, sacrifice, and wisdom. Many Amish practices appear cumbersome and pointless to modern Americans, but often they are a means of protecting their sense of family and community.

For example: The Amish see no evil in cars and tractors themselves, but they are careful to limit their use. They prefer to use horse-drawn vehicles of all shapes and sizes. Young people won't go as far from home in a buggy as they might in an automobile. The majority of Amish buggies have black tops. In Lancaster, Pennsylvania, they have gray tops. A small minority of Amish groups elsewhere use bright yellow, dark yellow, or white tops. Those who drive cars usually select a dark color—preferably black.

Dress among the Amish varies a great deal, but simplicity and nonconformity to the rest of society are the basic convictions. Modesty is stressed. Women and girls wear their hair long and cover their heads with a prayer veiling. Their handmade full-skirted dresses and aprons reach well below their knees and are closed with pins rather than buttons. In Lancaster, bright colors are traditional for women; in other areas, less so. More modern Amish groups permit prints in addition to solid-colored fabrics.

Men and boys dress in dark pants and coats, and wear broad-brimmed hats of felt or straw, depending on the weather. They avoid buttons because of their association with the large brass buttons worn by the military, who historically were their persecutors.

Old Order Amish groups do not use electricity from public utilities. They choose not to be dependent upon power sources managed by the secular world. They use gas lamps, batteries, generators, and equipment and appliances whose energy comes from natural gas or gasoline engines. Water and wind power are utilized a great deal. Horses are standard field equipment; tractors are used only for their engines, which power silo fillers and other belt-powered equipment. These generalities, of course, have many exceptions.

The Amish are not against education, but they have wanted to avoid the influence and de-personalization of large, consolidated schools of the public system. Amish schools, by contrast, are an extension of the home, and stress self-sufficiency, thoughtfulness, and wisdom. Amish children do attend public schools in rural areas where the schools are small and community-centered.

Other aspects of Amish life which contrast with general society are: 1) a stress on caring for one's own elderly, resulting in refusal, in most cases, to accept any government aid or Social Security; 2) a love of the land and the tilling of the soil, living close to the cycles and times of nature; 3) growing and preparing food using tasty recipes and wholesome ingredients; 4) the family as a vital unit of support for the society (divorce is not permitted); 5) "success" in the hectic, status-conscious society is replaced by a desire to serve and blend into one's community.

The Amish way is not a static culture. It represents a rich, vital alternative to the fragmented ways of many segments of modern society.

Author's Note

Every summer over eleven thousand city children enjoy a free two-week vacation in a peaceful rural setting as guests of volunteer families, including many Amish and Mennonite families in Pennsylvania and Virginia. Nicole in this book was one of those children. Host families represent a wide variety of people. In the beginning they were mostly farmers; today they are teachers, mechanics, shopkeepers, plumbers, ministers, carpenters, and doctors.

The program is sponsored by the Fresh Air Fund, a nonprofit organization in New York City that has been in continuous operation from 1877. Children are selected by thirty volunteer community agencies such as churches and neighborhood community centers in the five boroughs of New York City.